BIGOTRY & SYSTEMIC RACISM

SHORT ESSAYS ON BIGOTRY AS I SAW IT

1

This page intentionally blank

SECTION 1

SITUATIONS THAT I HAVE ENCOUNTERED

All Men Are Created Equal-

- US Declaration of Independence, 1776

Throughout my childhood, I lived in all white communities. I would hear the kids in school use prejudicial terms and I would ask my parents what these terms meant. They always said something like:

> *"This is a bad term, and it is not used by polite people. It is not right to use such a term."*

I never heard my parents use a racist term.

Our school was a consolidated district school and there were a small number of kids that came from a district called Tuttle Hill Road. This was a poor black farming community about 15 miles away. These kids were basically shunned in school with one exception. Ron, who was a super athlete was loved by everyone. When talking about Ron, you would hear statements like, "Oh, he is one of the good ones." Although, as far as I know, the other kids from this Tuttle Hill Road farming community were not persecuted, they were close to invisible.

Later, as an older child in high school, my sensitivity toward racial discrimination was coming more into awareness where I had to decide how to react when racist statements or jokes were made. At my first job, it was an all-white environment. During the seven years I worked there, I was only aware of one black person, out of a few hundred who worked in this seasonal employment company

I never had a friend or even a close acquaintance of color until I met a few college students who were in the same classes that I attended. Even then, we only saw each other in classes or lab sessions. We never had occasion to socialize.

After I graduated from college and began my work career, I ran into numerous incidents where discrimination was evident, often with a wink and a nod.

The stories in this book are a collection of situations where minorities were denied opportunity or otherwise dehumanized by some sort of a collective understanding by the white people in power. Included are a few situations of other forms of discrimination that I wanted to share. I am writing this book hoping that situations such as these can be recognized and challenged when they happen. We should make people uncomfortable when they make such statements. It does not have to be an argument or a fight, it can simply be something like,

"I am uncomfortable with that," or,

"I don't agree with you"

If we challenge bigotry, we can come a little closer to Thomas Jefferson's words which were written in 1776.

1

Racism in Valdosta, Georgia, in the early 1970's

Very early in my work career, I was responsible for certain decorative paint processes for exterior automotive trim. This job encompassed all the process controls surrounding chromium plating, anodizing, and painting.

I went to Valdosta, Georgia, to visit a factory responsible for some of our automotive trim products. This was a real eye opener. The factory had violated many of the process requirements our company expected of them. The workers were exposed to so many hazards. Chemical, fumes, direct injury, etc. The process was in disrepair and parts and processes were contaminated. It was my job to tell them what they had to improve to maintain their supplier status at our company. Because of the importance of this business, I was with an operations manager and the plant manager of this company.

As we were walking through the process, I saw a black man inside a recently emptied acid tank cleaning the sides and the bottom. The vapors were stifling to a passerby. The man in the tank was working in a cloud of fumes. I asked about the danger of that job and if they could do anything about it. The response? "That's n****r work.

I made profuse notes and planned to write my report and review it with their management in the morning. The plant manager, who picked me up in the morning for the ride to the factory, suggested we have dinner together. I agreed and we hopped in his car. He showed me the "other side of the tracks" using barely concealed racist statements.   We saw rows of shotgun houses that had vertical siding boards with cracks between them much like the siding on ramshackle barns.

Once away from the town, we were on a narrow road. We were approaching, from behind, a black woman with a bundle on her head. I think it was laundry. This plant manager honked his horn and swerved at her. She jumped in alarm and fell into a small grassy ditch alongside the road. The plant manager drove on, laughing and he expected me to laugh, which I didn't do. He seemed to think I would automatically feel the same way he did. He then said, "You have to keep them in control. Look in the glovebox and see what we do when they get out of line.

I opened the glovebox and there was a large pistol, I think it was a 45.

I did not make a fuss. I was too unsure of myself at that time. I just asked the guy to take me directly to my hotel and I said I must write the report.

Side note:
I told my superiors at work about the incidents, both in the factory and on the road. They did not want to take any action and they made me feel like it wasn't my place to make such observations. This supplier was a low-price bidder on this business, and they did not want to resource it to a more expensive supplier.

At this point in time, the automotive industry rewarded its purchasing managers on achieving low bids on a competitive basis. Jobs would be granted based on price alone. Once a new contract was made, the auto companies sent in quality specialists to evaluate the manufacturing process. If problems were found, it would be fought tooth and nail and many problems were never resolved. This was because to fix the problems, the low price could not be maintained.

I am talking about the late 1960's and 1970's here. As my career in the automotive industry progressed, this "low price" mentality slowly was modified because of customer dissatisfaction and warranty costs. By the first time I retired in 2005, Quality was the primary goal, After the quality and engineering requirements were met, then price was a consideration.

2

"Have you ever seen my wife?"

I had a coworker, Gene, who was an engineering supervisor while I was a quality control superintendent. This man was brilliant, friendly, helpful but highly prejudiced. In the 1960's he was sponsored by our company in drag racing, and he knew all the big names in this field. He was a very interesting guy and we talked quite a bit about his racing days.

The nature of our roles resulted in being together a lot and we often had lunch together in the company cafeteria. He talked quite a bit about his anger at the blacks who were fishing on the lake he lived on. He was enraged that he could see them from his living room window.

He got on an angry tirade about this at the cafeteria table with several co-workers at our table. He announced that he was selling his house because of the "problem."

Note: He eventually did sell his house because of his hatred for the people fishing in his view.

The N-word was flying in full racist fashion. Others at the table were visibly disturbed but looked down and said nothing. Finally, at a pause in Gene's rant, I pulled out my wallet, opened it up and reached inside. I said, "Gene, have you ever seen a photo of my wife?" My wife was not black, and I never said she was, but the implication was there. The effect this had on Gene was as if he had walked into a plate glass window. He stopped mid-thought and fell silent. We all picked up our trays and left. Gene never said anything to me about this. A few years later he met my wife at a retirement party and gave no signal of surprise that she was white.

3

Quality rejection.

For several years, I was a Quality
Superintendent in a large factory
producing OEM components for auto
assembly plants. One of our tasks was
to sample final product to see if it met
all the quality and performance
parameters that were specified by our
customers. I had many inspectors in
my group, and they were overseen by
27 salaried supervisors.

One of the best supervisors was a
woman of color named Eileen H. She
was very smart, knew her job and had
outstanding people skills. During her
job, she found a failure in which
production alternators to meet the
required performance specifications.
Since the alternators were 100% tested
for these characteristics The reasons

that these were not caught by the production process could be many. The most likely reasons were:

a) The in-process testers were improperly set up

b) Someone knowingly cheated because they would be in trouble for making a full day's production that would be rejected.

c) Damage occurred after the alternators passed the performance test.

This rejection started an angry storm of protest and name calling. At the end of each week, the area managers had to report their performance for the week. This would be a painful report in front of the plant manager, and it would likely impact the area manager's performance review and ultimately his bonus and salary.

The area manager, Ronald D. (Ron) talked to Eileen in an attempt to get her to pretend the rejection never happened. After she stood her ground, he aggressively questioned the inspector's ability, as well as Eileen's ability. They both stood fast and refused to OK the bad parts.

Later, toward the end of the day, Ron came into my office. This was a rare occurrence since we never liked each other. He made a big showing of closing my office door while telling me that he had to discuss something of importance with me. His initial statement was within earshot of others in the office area, then he closed the door.

Ron sat down across from my desk and started the conversation with, "Isn't Eileen H a dumb f***ing n*****?"

I was stunned. I knew Ron from other run-ins, and I had no doubt he had racist tendencies. I also knew he would cheat to pass off rejected components to prevent the rework or possible scrapping of parts. This, however, was full-blown undisguised hatred.

In the past, I heard him, in a group, use racist terms, in the form of jokes for co-workers. But this blatant assumption that such a tactic would work in this instance gave me pause to understand the depravity of what he was trying to do.
The only thing I said was, "Ron, Eileen is the best quality supervisor in this factory. She knows her job. I

stand behind her work. You and I do not see eye to eye in this situation and I, in no way, support your characterizing of people like that."

With that, Ron did not say a word. He stormed out & slammed the door

This brings us to the next chapter.

4

Human sacrifice

Early during the morning after the racist rant by Ronald D. over rejected alternators, Eileen came to me with a bunch of torn quality tags her inspector found in the trash. She then found out that the rejected alternators were illegally OK'd during the midnight shift and were shipped to the assembly plant. The papers she showed me were the torn-up reject tags that her inspector had written the day before. She delved into the shipping records and found out that one of Ron's production foremen, a Hispanic gentleman named John Castro, had fraudulently written OK tags for the entire group in question.

That day it was my turn to walk into Ronald D's office and close the door.

I presented him the evidence and asked him to explain it. I told him I knew John Castro and I always considered him to be hard-working and honest.

Confronted with the evidence, Ron told me, "If you wish to pursue this, I will call John Castro into the office and fire him on the spot – right in front of you. Otherwise, get the f*** out of my office." As I left, I told Ron that this was brinksmanship, and I did not appreciate it.

I walked out steaming with anger. I went to my boss and told the entire story, including the threat to fire John Castro who, I believed, was told to write the OK tags or else lose his job.

My boss, who was friendly with Ron, did not escalate the situation either higher in the organization or directly with Ron. When I look back at this, I see my actions as a failure because I did not take the issue either to our Human Relations department, or to corporate levels.

Final note: About 2 years later, I was shopping in town, and I ran into John Castro. I had never talked to him about the ugly situation where his job was on the line either way. John, with strong emotion, told me, "Marc, I want to thank you for saving my job." I never was sure what exactly he knew about the interactions we had with Ronald D, but he somehow felt I was responsible for his not being fired. (Note 1) I think the actual language was so reprehensible that I chose to mask it with asterisks.

5

5

Racist cop

When our kids were in high school, we attended quite a few football and basketball games. It was lots of fun as some of the players were friends with our kids. At every event, there was assigned the same County Sheriff. He was would freely interact with students and parents. He was well known, and all the kids and parents loved this guy. We all called him by his first name, Chip.

One day at work, I went to a nearby fast-food place to get a sandwich. Chip was there and we ate lunch together. After that, Chip would call me on the occasion he was in the area, and we would have lunch together. I truly liked the guy. One time when I returned from Europe on a business trip, Chip happened to be there. The police were watching closely for drugs, and we had to go through a line where dogs would sniff the bags. If the dog sat down by a bag, you were in for a detailed search.

When Chip saw me, he came up to me and walked me around the complete line to the exit of the terminal. At the time, I was gratified, and I thought to myself, what a good thing it is to have Chip as a friend. I did not think about how this privilege was only extended to a friend of a cop and how unfair that was.

The last time I saw Chip, he told me he does not have enough action in Washtenaw County (Michigan). He was arranging a transfer back to Wayne County which includes Detroit. I was surprised and I asked him why he would want to do that as I thought he had an ideal job assignment. He told me he wanted some action and he wanted to "Bust some n****r heads." (Exact words).

To my detriment, I did not say anything. I was shocked that this guy that I really liked, and everyone loved was such an open racist using the power of the Sheriff's office to abuse people of color. I told my wife about the incident, and she found it upsetting for the same reasons. I never saw Chip again.

6

Racism next door in Dundee Michigan.
_~1964_

When I was in college, I had a chemistry lab course which had a black student, James, in the class. I was taking chemistry and math courses and especially at that time it was rare that any of my courses included a black student. We chatted during our chemistry lab work, and he was really a nice guy. I never socialized with him, but then since I was working and living off campus I did not socialize with any students. During the summers, I would work two jobs to try to get ahead financially.

On one summer weekend day, while visiting my dad and stepmother, there was a knock on the front door. I went to see who it was and to my surprise, there stood James, my college lab friend. We both were surprised to see each other. As it turned out, he was selling encyclopedias hoping to get enough money to return to college in the fall.

Since Dundee, Michigan, at that time, was an all-white community with very little tolerance for minorities, I asked him what his level of reception and success was in door to door selling. He said it was generally cool with doors quickly closed.

I told him I was visiting my parents and not in a position to buy. We chatted for several minutes about things we had in common in our chemistry labs, about the professors, and Eastern Michigan University in general.

As we chatted, I saw a lady come to the sidewalk in front of our house and fold her arms and glare at us. It was our next-door neighbor, Mrs. K. She stood there all the time James was on our porch. She never said a word, but her glare was angry and unflinching. James and I both agreed this was a hostile situation.

James went along house to house to try to earn a few bucks and Mrs. K turned her glare to follow him as he walked away. Neither James nor I said anything to her, and she did not speak to us.

I grew up knowing the "K" family since Mr. K had a furniture store in Dundee. In fact, some of our furniture was purchased at their store. I always admired the family as they had a thriving business and appeared to be one of the leading citizens of our small community.

In an all-white environment, you have no way to gage people's prejudices until there is an opportunity, such as James' visit, for these racists have a chance to display their intolerance.

7

Is "Polack" a bad word?

My maternal grandfather was named Ed Szarkowski. He was born in the early 1880's and he was 60 years old when I was born. He was my best friend from my earliest memories through my early teens. I was 6 years old when we lived in Humbird, Wisconsin where my father had a cheese factory. Our grandparents lived in the nearby Polish settlement of Lublin, Wisconsin, about 45 miles North of Humbird.

As far back as I can remember, he referred to people of Polish ancestry as "Polacks." It seemed as natural as calling someone English, Spanish, or French.

When we moved to Dundee Michigan in the late 1940's, Grandpa Ed and Grandma May moved there with us. There were quite a few Polish families in Dundee, and they were friends with us as well as with our grandparents.

One time when I was around 8 years old, Grandpa Ed came to our house visibly sad. He said, "I never knew that 'Polack' was a bad word." It turned out that he used that term and received a tongue-lashing and was told it was improper to use such a word.

This was at a time when mainstream white America was almost totally insensitive to anything that singled out immigrants and/or minorities. I remember my 8-year-old reasoning - thinking, "People can call me a Polack all day long. It doesn't bother me."

Now, I think the person that pointed out that such a word shouldn't be used was brave because there certainly wasn't support for such a correction. This label is a form of discrimination and we all should politely tell people when they are making the mistake of ethnic labeling.

8

Bowser the racist dog

When my older brother, Russ and
I were around 9 and 7 years old,
we had a dog show up in our
yard. He adopted us. We named
him Bowser. We were told that
the dog was a Belgian Bouvier as
evidenced by his appearance and
specifically because the inside of
his mouth was black.

Back then, dogs ran free, and it
was generally accepted unless
they presented a danger or
otherwise caused a concern.
Bowser was very protective and
was our constant companion
whether in our yard, in the
nearby woods or camping.

Our house was at the edge of town. Across the railroad tracks was Karner Brothers grain elevator. Every Saturday during harvest time, tractors pulling wagons full of grain were lined up along our street waiting to deliver their crops to the grain elevator.

Most of the farmers were white and we would set up Kool-Aid© stand and sell cold drinks to the farmers who were in line and waiting. There was a black farming community in the nearby area and occasionally a black farmer would be in line.

Our dog went ballistic every time he saw a person of color. This was a rare occasion, but it was a dangerous situation as he displayed all the signs of a serious attack, and he was big enough to do real harm. He never displayed such a threat to white strangers. He would bark at any stranger but if they approached, he would be totally friendly.

A local Dundee resident said he knew the person that previously had Bowser (who named him "Jack") and he was racist and trained the dog to attack blacks. Whenever we wanted to reprimand Bowser, we found that calling him "Jack" made him (afraid?) and he would obey our commands.

9

Philadelphia jazz club

I have always loved Jazz. As a
pre-school child, I remember my
parents having jazz records
which they played on a large
standing walnut combination
radio and record player. As I
grew older, I listened to a 5-tube
clock radio, and I found out I
could tune into jazz programs
from far away by "skips" of AM
radio waves after complete
darkness.

On an early work trip, I was sent
to Philadelphia to take a
technical course. After the
coursework, I went to the
downtown hotel where I was
staying and had dinner. I

decided to walk around the area and while still on the street, I heard good jazz music coming from a bar. I thought, "How lucky can I be?" I decided to go in and order a beer and nurse it for a long time so I could hear the music.

I was still wearing my work attire, a suit, white shirt & tie. I walked in the door and the lights were low. I couldn't see much but there was a bar close to the door, so I went in to take a seat at that bar. It was then that I noticed everyone in the bar was black. A lot of the patrons were staring at me. No one was dressed like me. I did not know how to react. I said to the bartender that I would like a beer. He said, "You had better walk out that door you just came in … RIGHT NOW (with heavy emphasis)."

I walked out and nothing else was said. Once on the street, it was like "Did I imagine that?" "Was it a threat or was it just so unusual that it caught people off guard?"

After that incident, I slowly came to the realization that this situation, which I had never experienced or even imagined before, is something that minorities go through on a regular basis.

10

Grandma Szarkowski

Early in my first marriage, we
visited my aged grandmother, born
in 1880. We had not seen each
other for around 10 years. She was
upset because when my mother
died, my dad remarried a non-
Catholic. Her position on this
became unbearable and we just
avoided her.

When our daughters were around 4
and 6 years old, we decided they
should see their grandmother. She
loved them and it was a warm
reunion. Toward the end of the
visit, she expressed some general
fear of black people. We were
shocked and gave a mild pushback
saying that we have some friends of
color, and we did not agree with

generalizations. She then said, "You know, black people come from monkeys. They have tails. They just hide them." This poor woman spent the rest of her time without seeing her great grandchildren.

11

We have this town "tied up."

When we were buying the rural 20 acres for our first house, we went to Barry, a local land broker that we knew. Nancy, my wife had worked for Barry in the past, and he was friendly to us to a fault. He seemed to be the greatest friend in the area. He continued to visit from time to time and he loved our daughters. He became a grandfatherly figure to them, and we were always happy to see him.

Barry was a prominent citizen of a small town. He had connections with business owners, lawyers, judges, and even the undertaker. This group of people, as I found out, pretty much controlled the development of the town.

Quite some time after we bought the land and built the house, he stopped by as he occasionally did. He said he wanted to talk to me about something important. Barry became unusually serious and asked me if we were thinking of selling the house. I told him that this was not something we were considering. Regardless, he gave me a stern word of warning: "We have this town sewed up. If you ever sell to an undesirable, you will be in big trouble, and no one will help you. If ever decide to sell your house, you must contact us, first. We will sell it and see that we maintain our community. "

Up to that point, I had never suspected there would be a mean bone in Barry's body. This warning left me confused and I asked him what he meant. He simply repeated the warning and told me that I must see him first if I decide to sell. I then understood this to be an open threat with no provocation. He was offering a carrot and stick approach: (We'll sell it sell for good price") and ("You will be in trouble if you sell to an 'undesirable'") approach. Barry and I never discussed this again.

We remained "friendly" with Barry for more than 30 years until the time of his death. This was never brought up again.

12

Deeply embedded southern racism

My first job after college was with
Wyandotte Chemical Company. They
gave me a prestigious title, especially
for a fresh college graduate. I was
working as a research staff member.
Wyandotte made many diversified
products used in institutions. I was
working in the Laundry Products
Division. There were three Research
Staff Members and two outstanding
Research technicians (one of which
has become a lifelong best friend.)

The other technician, Tim M. was
from Mississippi, and he was very
friendly and worked with the team
without flaw. He was irritating
because his speech often drifted into
ugly racist remarks.

One day, at lunch, Tim went on a racist rant about a traffic incident. Something we would now call road rage. I asked Tim why he went out of his way to speak so disparagingly about black people. I pointed out that he does not speak about conflicts with white people that way.

Tim said, and this is an exact quote: "Listen. My granddaddy hated N*****s; My daddy hated N*****s; And I am always going to hate N*****s.

This response left me speechless. As it turned out, I got a job offer from another company about that time and I do not know whether Tim ever tempered his hatred.

13

Sexual harassment in the factory.

One summer, I had the pleasant experience of hiring a young woman engineering student for an internship in an integrated manufacturing and design group. _(Note: Integrated in this sense meant that both the design engineers and the manufacturing engineers reported to me)._

The intern, Beverly, was an indigenous Native American who was born into a tribal community in Central America. She was adopted at 5 years old by American parents and they gave her an environment where she could excel in most anything she wanted. She was a third-year student at Purdue University when I met her. She was very good at her job. She was popular with our team members, and she willingly jumped into a situation to help.

At the end of her internship, we had an exit interview. I told Beverly that I appreciated here knowledge and work ethic. I asked her if she would consider coming back to our company after she graduated.

Beverly became uneasy and finally told me "I would never consider working here." I asked her why and she was very reluctant to say anything. I finally coaxed out of it that someone in the factory kept feeling her up.

This was unbelievable and I asked her, "Was it one of our team members?" She emphatically said that it wasn't, but she would not tell me anymore.

We had an hourly person, Gary B., assigned to our group to assist with statistical data collection. Gary was boisterous and he was full of unbelievable stories (aka lies) about his current influence with the military. I immediately suspected Gary, but I had no proof.

I asked Gary to come into my office. He sat down across from my desk. I stared at him for about 20 seconds. He became uncomfortable, then I said, "Beverly told me all about what happened."

At that, Gary fidgeted for about a minute and started and stopped sentences not really saying anything. I just waited. Finally, he said, "I was just massaging her back. I thought she liked it." Gary began crying.

With that, I told Gary, "These people are not here for your personal pleasure.

I am going to see to it that you are fired.

I then went to the manufacturing manager who was responsible for Gary's job assignments. In doing this, I bypassed a foreman and a superintendent. The Manufacturing Manager, a woman, said, "What do you expect me to do about it? I'm busy and have a job to do." With that she asked me to leave.

I then went to our Human Relations Department where the matter was taken very seriously, and Gary was fired.

Sadly, after a period, I don't know if it was 30 or 60 days, the union went to bat for Gary, and he was reinstated.

14

I was accused of racism.

Sadly, this was one of the most challenging situations I ran into as a supervisor, and it bothered me for several years.

This another story that happened when I was the supervisor of an integrated engineering team. Again, "integrated" in this sense means that both manufacturing engineering and design engineering were in the same group.

We had a manufacturing line that was making small DC electric motors for automotive use. This was a new project was developed from concept to production. The project became a reality when our company bought the design of the electric motor from another company and in that respect, we had a lot of interfaces, and we were greatly aided by their experience.

As this manufacturing line went into full production, we needed to hire more engineers to further develop both the process and the design. I was given the resume of a young engineer from a different division of our company.

He looked like he would be a great addition to our team. His past performance review was "Outstanding,"" the highest performance praise given by our company.

Reece's first assignment was to work with two other experienced team members to get to know both the process and the design. Our intention was to give him a direct assignment when he felt comfortable, or in about 3-6 months. Reece was very popular. He was open and friendly, and everyone liked him.

I soon became aware that Reece was following the other engineers in a passive manner. When we had meetings, he would defer any question to one of his other team members. When pressed directly, he could not answer the questions. I finally concluded that the other engineers were covering for him by helping him with even the most basic aspects of his assignments, data analysis and report writing.

I had a performance review with Reece after 1 year and I told him that he needed to break out and utilize his engineering skills. At this point, Reece told me that he was very unsure of his engineering ability. He began sobbing when he told me this. He went on to say that he went to college in a small school where his father was the dean. Reece, however, was one of few black students. He said he was popular, but all his friends were white. He went on to admit that he was afraid of the black kids. I told Reece that I would give him a satisfactory review, but I wanted to work directly with him to improve his performance. He was elated with this offer. I said we would have a review every 3 months for the next year to make sure we both agreed on the progress.

After Reece's performance review, I called the previous supervisor who had rated him "outstanding." This guy had the nerve to tell me that Reece was one of the poorest engineers he had ever seen. I became angry and asked, "Why the hell did you give him an outstanding performance review?" I was told words to the effect, "Look, If I gave him the review he deserved, no one would want him, and I'd be stuck with him." There were only a handful of times I used profanity in my job, but this was one of them.

Reece continued to go to other engineers to have them do simple tasks. It was mostly the simple math used for statistical control and basic engineering disciplines such as tolerance stackups and other such math-related tasks. Most of these could be easily done on a spreadsheet, but Reece simply could not do them.

At our interim performance review, after 3 months, I told Reece, that I was changing his assignment. I was expecting him to attend engineering meetings and bring back all the assignments our group would be responsible for, so I could hand these assignments to the right engineers. Reece attended several and came back without notes and no ability to identify the assignments.

I met with him again and said I would go to the next meeting with him and take notes. I expected him to also take notes and write the report and we would compare our assignment list.

After that meeting, Reece did not have his report on time. I told him I needed his report by the close of business. He then asked me for my notes. I asked him to first see his notes and he did not have any.

I talked this over with my management and with Human Relations. They were made aware of the prior supervisor's remarks and all the struggles to perform. We agreed that I would give him another interim performance review and downgrade him and tell him improvement was needed if he were to remain working for our company.

At that point, Reece became angry. Perhaps more alarmed than angry. He shouted at me and said this review was a lynching. I responded and said that the word "Lynching" is a very coded word and I resented that he used it to help explain his bad performance, especially after months of working together to identify issues and improve his performance.

Reece went to Human Relations and accused me of racism. This was a stinging blow to me, and I talked to them about it. They told me that once this type of charge is made, they must give him another assignment with someone else who will watch his performance closely and give him quarterly reviews.

Within a year after Reece was reassigned to another area within the factory, he was fired for poor performance. Specifically for poor engineering skills and total lack of follow up on meetings.

To this day I wish that I could have helped him.

15

Anti-Asian prejudice

In my first job working for a major automotive company, I was lucky enough to be the only chemist in a lab that needed chemists. At the same time, we were bringing in a lot of analytical instrumentation. I loved it and my boss seemed to really appreciate me.

One day a new guy showed up in the lab. Our supervisor was on vacation the week before and prior to his vacation, he had interviewed this man and turned him down. Management had hired him anyway because the guy's credentials were solid. When John, our supervisor, came to work he went on a rant. He fired this guy and took him to Human Relations to have him escorted out of the building. They were gone for a few hours which was an unexpectedly long time

to walk a fired employee to Human
Relation.

The next development was that our
supervisor, John, and the new employee,
Edward, came back and Edward was given a
desk and an assignment. John was red-faced
and said very little.

About a week later, Edward came his desk
at 7:50 AM, which was 10 minutes before
starting time. John became enraged and
took him to Human Relations for being late.
I should note that 10 minutes before starting
time was not unusual for other employees.
John argued (note 1) that a person cannot be
at work with only 10 minutes to start time
and then be in the lab working by start time.
This was a truly stupid argument, but John
scared me so much that I developed a
pattern of coming in 30 minutes early
because there was no reasoning with this
man.

Edward and I worked closely together, and he was a nice guy. We got to know and like each other. Our supervisor, John, was often gruff with Edward. He sometimes would criticize his work in front of others and to me it seemed unfair. Edward was often singled out for criticism.

Note 1: I later got to know the manager of the department and we discussed this situation with John and Edward. The manager told me that John was on "Thin ice" and inferred that he would have been demoted if he had not transferred to a different location.

16

Anti-gay prejudice

(This event is not about racial prejudice; it is about anti-gay prejudice.)

Ben was a good friend whom I worked with for years. He was a lifelong comedian and his turn on many events resulted in lots of laughter. He was truly a nice guy.

Ben occasionally made jokes at the expense of gay people. He knew that I had friends and some family members who were gay. His jokes were not the horrible ones, but nevertheless, he felt enough hostility toward gays (my opinion) that he was comfortable putting them down.

When I had a milestone birthday, my wife, Madelon, arranged for a party in which she invited a group of friends, including Ben, my work friend. I was a little uneasy about this because we would have a couple, two gay men, present who are among our best friends.

Before the party, I talked to Ben. I made him aware of the gay couple and I told him, "I know you have issues with gay couples, and I wanted to give you a "heads-up" that this couple will be at the party too. Ben made a brief joke, but then said, "Don't worry, I'll be OK with them."

At the party, our two friends were seated at a table when Ben arrived. Ben took the empty chair next to the couple and I was watching and not seeing any sign of negative behavior by Ben.

As the party progressed, Ben and the couple got into discussions that were lively and happy. I was also happy because the meeting of my friends with Ben went much better than I expected.

The following Monday, at work, I sought out Ben.   I mentioned that he seemed to be getting along very well with my two friends.

Ben was silent for a few seconds, then his eyes turned upward as if he was looking at the ceiling. His words still ring in my ears:

"Sometimes it is different when you put a face on it."

I was astonished and I passed this along to the couple who met Ben. I think Ben's admission was also evidence of never having an acquaintance with someone who is gay.   I also think this "isolation" is something that is a driving force for most forms of prejudice.

17

We love you but you can't live in our town.

In our high school, there were no white teachers. Eventually, they hired a black band teacher, and he was good. Everyone loved him. He routinely drove the 45-mile trip from Ann Arbor, Michigan to Dundee. At one point, he decided that he was so well accepted that he should buy a house and be part of the community.

During the house hunt, he was met with strong opposition from some of the townspeople who were clearly racist. As a result, he gave up the search for a house and continued to make the drive daily.

One winter day, he got into an automobile accident and died as a result.

There was an outpouring of grief from the people of town. A town that collectively loved his expertise at teaching music, but felt he was not worthy of living within our all-white borders.

18

White privilege – early awareness

While working my way through College, I needed money badly. I had one low paying job for 7 years after high school, but I decided to try for a second job in a factory during my second summer.

I applied for an hourly job at a local Ford factory. Even though they had a large stack of applicants, I had heard that if you show up in the morning, you can get a job because they needed someone for that day.

Around the third day of showing up and being discouraged by the guy behind the window, I saw a man, who turned out to be a foreman, holding a piece of paper and talking to the person who does the hiring.

At the time, there were three black guys and me eagerly looking for work.

The door opened and the foreman looked at the three black guys, then he looked at me. He pointed toward me and said, "You, come on in here."

I was hired that day and the other guys were not even considered.

Even though I was elated to get the job, when I looked back and knew it was because I was white. My ideas of how prejudice works were not very sophisticated at the time – but I knew.

19

The Nazi next door

Somewhere around 1972, I visited a good friend and past co-worker in a nearby suburb of Detroit, Michigan. Lorenzo and his new wife, Beverly had bought a nice house about a year prior, and we were eager to see their new surroundings. The house and yard were well cared for and we were happy for them to have such a nice place.

Lorenzo and I walked into his back yard. It was fenced with a see-through (I think chain link) fence of about 5 ft high. A man was in the next yard and Lorenzo cautioned me that he was an open Nazi. The next thing I knew, Lorenzo said "Hi" to him and the neighbor came over to the fence. The neighbor had a large, threatening German shepherd that was intent on attacking us both but for the fence. Lorenzo, for some reason, introduced me as "Marc Rosenstein."

The neighbor's demeanor changed from neutral to mean in a flash. He said, "Oh! A Jew-boy, huh?" I felt he was ready to mix it up physically if I were to escalate it.

Lorenzo laughed and said words to the effect, "Calm down, he is not Jewish, I just wanted to show him how you would react."

That was the end of my conversation with this ugly Nazi. Problems existed however, with Lorenzo and Beverly. Lorenzo and Beverly could not enjoy their back yard because of the threat of the German shepherd. Later, after our visit to their new house, I was surprised that they moved. The neighbor's threats were magnified by the German shepherd getting out of the yard and biting Beverly.

I found out much later, that upon moving into their new house, Lorenzo was doing some interior work and needed some sort of tool that he did not have with him. He asked Beverly to introduce herself to the guy next door and see if he had a tool he could lend them.

By a strange coincidence, the neighbor at their new house was a Nazi who had a German shepherd. The dog got out and bit Beverly.

Lorenzo and Beverly remain in the new house and the Nazi has moved away.

20

The Rosemarie ordeal

(This is a story about misogyny and coercion)

In my work career, I always loved my job. I had a few bosses I did not like and there is a big difference which I will illustrate below.

Quite early in my career, I was made supervisor over a group of analysts. These people were devoted and hard working. Their principal task was to analyze automobile warranty and find the root causes of problems people were having with our vehicles. Then they participated in the effort to make corrective actions in design, manufacturing, or both.

This was an experience group. They readily accepted me when I became their supervisor. Things were going well for me, and I think also for the group.

About a year into this job, my boss requested that I hire a certain woman into my group from another similar group which was working on a different product line.

This woman, Rosemarie, had a bad reputation. The stories were rampant that she was having an affair with my boss who was married. I checked with the woman's supervisor, and I was told that she didn't care to learn her job and she flaunted her relationship with the manager, also my boss.

I tried to tactfully decline my boss's request. I told him we have enough people in the group to meet all our assignments. He told me to find some assignments for her. He went on to say that she was being treated unfairly in the other group and he was just trying to give her a fair chance.

I told my boss, Rob, I was aware of the relationship between him and Rosemarie. I said I felt that would put me in a very uncomfortable position. Rob told me that if I hired her, he would never intervene in any way regarding how I managed and rated her.

I still said "no," but the next thing, Rob told the Human Relations department that she was moving into my group. I was not happy but tried to make the best of it.

Rosemarie's job involved the precise measuring of engineered components. She did not have a clue about the use of calipers or micrometers. I sent her to a Chicago class on using basic measuring instruments. She never attended but used the opportunity to shop. (I had other people in the class, so I knew this with certainty.)

The entire group struggled with Rosemarie. She was disruptive. There were times when she disagreed with the entire group. These times would be followed by a phone call to me from Rob asking what is going on.

In one incident, I was giving Rosemarie a performance review in my office with the door closed. Before we could get into the review she reached across the desk, rubbed my arm, and said, "Wouldn't it be funny if you and I had an affair?"

My immediate reaction was to calmly tell her that I had too much to lose and said we should get on with the performance review.

I then excused myself and opened the door. There was one analyst working at his desk and I asked him to come to the desk just outside my office and be witness if anything happened.

I tthen told Rosemarie I was taking her down one performance level rating and that could be short term if she overcame her deficiencies with measurement and reporting.

With the threat of a bad performance review, she got up and screamed at her loudest voice, "You can take this Goddamned job and shove it up your f*****g ass" (actual quote.) She then stormed out of the office. I could see people gathering in the halls talking about what just happened.

About an hour later, I got called into my boss's office. He was red faced and angry. He asked me why I am treating her unfairly. I tried to tell him what happened. He wasn't listening. I did not tell him about the comment about an affair. Rob was having none of my comments. He went on to tell me that I was deficient in performance, and he was going to have me go to rudimentary classes as a condition of my keeping my job.

This surprised me as, before this incident, he had been very complimentary regarding my performance and he I gave me the highest performance ratings for a few years.

Rob was so worked up that I wondered if he was going to get into a physical altercation with me. I then did something I knew was wrong, but I did it anyway. I shook my finger very close to his face and said, "Rob, you spend more time with her than I do." With that he exploded and ran out of the office. His secretary had already run out of the office.

The next thing, I was called into the Human Relations Department to explain my side of what happened. To my amazement, they believed my explanation because of past disturbances caused by Rob interfering with Rosemarie's job assignments and ratings. I went further. I let them know I was going to file an official charge of nepotism.

The HR guy, a nice person, told me, "You can't file a nepotism charge because they don't live together." With that, I pulled out a photocopy made from a paper dictionary that defined nepotism and handed it to him. It made no mention of living together. He asked me to hold off on making a charge and that he would talk to the plant manager and get back to me right away.

The Human Relations person, after talking to the plant manager, said words to the effect:

> "Look, we are aware of what Rob has been doing. He has had similar issues in the past. We trust you. We ask that you do not file the charge, and in turn we will relocate Rosemarie and we will deal with Rob. We meet every Friday, and I will give you a verbal update with each meeting."

It took a long time, but they were good to their word. First, they offered Rosemarie to a long-term friend of mine who was a supervisor in another plant. I told the friend to not take her and why I felt that way.

Finally, she was moved to another group. As for Rob, he was punished by a demotion from a plant Quality Manager to a supervisor of mechanics in a company garage. Shortly after that, Rob left the company, of his own accord.

I liked Rob. Prior to this incident we worked well together. Just before he left the company, Rob called me to see how I was doing. I never expected such a call. We chatted for a few minutes and Rob was very friendly. I thought it was his way of trying to apologize for the trouble he caused.

I said to him, "It was unfortunate that you and I got into such a troubling situation, but I hope thing are going well for you. To my amazement, Rob said "What trouble? What are you talking about?"

I gave a much too long of a pause and we ended the conversation with pleasantries. I was wondering if Rob was suffering from some form of dementia. Shortly after that phone call, Rob left the company and died a few years afterwards of a disease other than dementia.

SECTION 2

OTHER BRIEF, BUT NOTABLE, EXPERIENCES

21

Racist grandmas

In my first marriage, we had to explain to our then young children that their maternal great-grandma's calling of Brazil nuts "n***** toes" was a bad thing.

In another instance, their paternal great-grandmother told our daughters that black people "Have tails, but they hide them."

22

Another Nazi

In college, I had a roommate, Tom, who befriended an avowed Nazi. This was after Tom and I roomed together and the Nazi, Mitch, was then rooming with Tom.

Mitch openly hated everything. He talked primarily about his hatred of Jews and black people, but many other groups were targets for him. This was the first of three people I met that felt comfortable spewing filth. Tom and I did not have much to do with each other after my first meeting with Mitch.

I told another friend, "Someday, we will read about Mitch in the newspapers." That never happened but he was certainly a candidate for violence.

23

Send defective parts to Mexico

Early in my career, I was working in a quality laboratory at and automotive production facility, we found brake master cylinders which had a severe safety defect: Porosity in the cylinder bore. This porosity could tear up a rubber seal and leave the car without braking ability.

The Area manager said, "We'll ship these to the f*****g Mexicans. To my amazement, they were shipped to an assembly plant in Mexico, and we never heard about these defective parts again.

24

A "Pushy" misogynist

At one point, the engineering group that I was responsible for had designed and ordered a special cleaning chamber for small DC electric motor components. When the project was near completion, I sent a top-notch female engineer to the facility to review the unit's performance as a step before shipping it to our facility.

When she returned, she was obviously upset. I asked her what that was all about, and she told me that the owner of the supplying company was aggressive toward her, and she did not want to go back. She told me that he stepped on her toes and was pushing her shoulders back, threatening that he was going to make her fall.

I had a hard time believing her story wasn't exaggerated, but I could not let it go without checking it out. I called the guy. Even over the phone, he was loud and bullying. He gave me enough information that I knew that the reported incident was true. He was then angry at me because I called him about the incident.

I passed this information on to our department that approves equipment suppliers in the hopes they would be disqualified from further bids.

25

"What ARE you?"

I sent a female Asian Indian to a plant
in central Indiana with a routine
process-related assignment. She had
been the plant before, and people there
knew her. As she was walking down
the main aisle in the plant, an hourly
machine operator left his job, walked
up to her.

He asked her, "What are you?"

She said she was an engineer
from central offices and was here
to review a project.

He said, "I know that but what
ARE you?"

She said, "if you are wondering about my ethnicity, I am an Asian Indian."

With that, he turned around and went back to his job.

26

"Are you a Jew, an Arab or what?"

I was with a group of engineers traveling during a time of severe middle east turmoil. We were waiting for our next flight and watching the developing news on the airport TV. Within our group was a smaller man who was of Pakistani origin.

A large man came up to our Pakistani co-worker and, unbelievably, shoved him. He said, "Are you a Jew an Arab or what?" Immediate rescue was performed by a giant among us. Our intervening co-worker was 6'8" and was a college football player. Big John said, "What seems to be the trouble here?" The aggressor took one look and ran away without another word.

There was nothing that any of our group did to egg this guy on. He was seething with anger over the breaking news and took it out on someone small and whose appearance suggested he was Middle Eastern.

27

Unfounded fear No. 1

During a manpower planning session, our director suggested that a fellow supervisor of mine, Perry, take an engineer, named Travis, into his group.

Travis worked with me in the past and he was an outstanding engineer who got along with everyone. He was Jamaican, very tall, and dark complexioned. Travis was also assertive without being aggressive.

The supervisor became visibly shaken. He started rubbing his hands together and showed other stress signs. He told the director that Travis scared him, and he felt Travis was way too "militant" and aggressive.

The Director, also a minority, let Perry's assertions of fear go without challenge.

28

Unfounded fear No. 2

For more than 15 years, I have met
(and still meet) with a small group of
friends most Saturdays for breakfast.
This includes my older brother Russ
and some other close friends. We have
a good time and friendly chats. It is a
good way to keep in touch.

At one time, we invited a new member
to this group. He could meet only
during the summer months since he
spent the winters in Arizona. He often
complained about the Mexicans who
he saw as responsible for a crime wave
in Arizona. He cited the fact that the
jails were full of these "Dangerous
undocumented Mexicans."

It was true that the jails were full of
arrested illegal aliens who were
crossing the border to get jobs. We

pointed out that the cause of the high number of arrests was due to the racist Maricopa County Sheriff, Joe Arpaio. This made national news and Arpaio was racially profiling and arresting illegal immigrants. The bulk of those jailed was for the crime of having entered the country illegally.

This was a "crime" tolerated for decades as it was a necessary source of low-cost labor primarily for the farming industry. It was a known fact that the violent crime for the group of illegal immigrants was lower than the general population. The last thing they wanted to do was to bring police attention to themselves.

29

Racist beliefs about I.Q.

I had a manager who would repeatedly inject into the conversation his belief that black people were inferior intellectually. When anyone would tell him that he was wrong and his comments were based on bigotry, he would cite numbers from a book he had read and apparently memorized.

Also in our office was a PhD statistician who was black. One day this statistician happened to be passing by our office when our manager was loudly claiming white superiority.

The statistician, without visible signs of anger, told our boss that he was citing a disproven and racist author and the statistics cited were completely wrong.

Our manager, completely embarrassed, did not drop his racist views, but he never again talked about it when he was in an open office situation.

30

Open ridicule of minorities

In one of my early (Mid 1980's) assignments, I was a superintendent in a factory. Within our office, we had about seven superintendents, one of which, George, was black.

The entire office and upper management, including the plant manager, would often make fun of George. Typically, we would have a production level meeting to discuss developments or problems and each superintendent would have to discuss his operation for a few minutes.

When George gave his presentation, you could see people glancing at each other in a manner that was not respectful. On occasion, when the meeting ended, the people that stayed behind would belittle George and use the N-word. This disrespect was in front of the Plant Manager, and it was never discouraged.

31

Failure to challenge racism.

As part of a major push into new business, I was part of a visit to a corporate plant in Monterrey, Mexico. We were a group of 6 people, and our most senior person was a woman who was the Business Unit Manager of our portion of bringing new cars into production.

The morning of our visit, we were greeted, and a short presentation was given to us about the Monterrey factory's preparation for the new business. After the meeting we were invited to the production operation to see for ourselves what was described in the earlier meeting.

One within our group was a black woman engineer, Linda. As we were getting ready to proceed to the production floor, Linda was told she cannot go with the group. When asked why, they said it was because she did not have the required safety shoes.

Linda's shoes were normal shoes, not open toed and not canvass or tennis-type shoes. No one in our group had safety shoes, including are Business Unit Manager.

To my astonishment, our leader, did not take any exception to the exclusion of Linda. On the flight home, our manager said words to the effect that "It was a critical sourcing trip, and she did not want to rock the boat."

32

Retirees revealing racist beliefs

Quite a while after I retired, I was invited to have breakfast monthly with a group of men that I worked with. I thought this would be a great way to keep in touch with old friends and I was eager to make this part of my routine.

This was during the time that Barack Obama was running for president. During my first two breakfast meetings, there were racist comments and jokes about Obama. When such jokes were told, more than half of the group of around 12 would laugh heartily and the others had various degrees of uncomfortableness.

I quit going to the meetings. I could not believe these people I worked with were so open with their racism.

Final Note:

I am lucky. I owe a lot to my parents, Roger and Martha Possley. As I grew up, I never heard them use racist terms. Whenever I asked them about some racist statement I heard, they told me that it was wrong, and they told me why.

To my knowledge, they never had black friends and we lived in a small all-white community, but mom & dad gave us a good foundation to face the world and recognize racial prejudice when we see it.

TABLE OF CONTENTS

Check out these other books by Marc Possley

Available on Amazon

TALES OF WAR
&
Related Stories
$11.95 paperback
$5.95 Kindle

———

Images in Black and White
Everyday objects revealed
As things of beauty
$15.95 paperback
$9.99 Kindle

———

TEAM ORIENTED
PROBLEM SOLVING
PART 2
Roadmap for Brainstorming:
Find and correct both
The
Process and the System Root Cause
$11.95 Amazon

Made in the USA
Columbia, SC
01 October 2021